C000156222

MTN BONDED

written by BROOKE MURDOCK

illustrated by AMY BUNNELL JONES

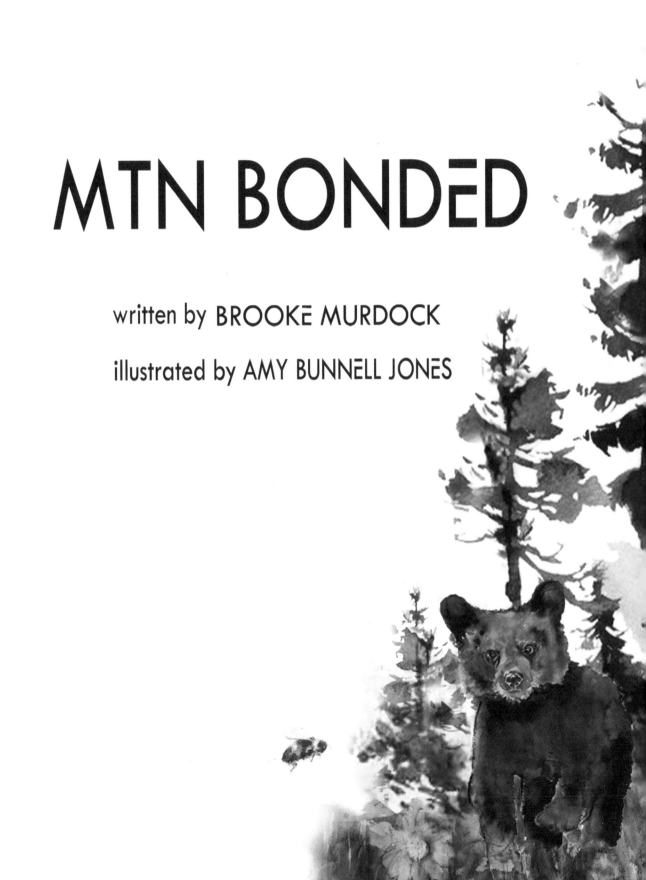

For my family and all those who love God's beautiful creations- Scarlet, McCray, Jack, Madi, Kai, Vivie, Kate, and Blakely
-BM

For my husband and soulmate, Michael. We share a love of nature, the same birthday, our desserts, and five amazing children.
-A.J.

Copyright 2020
Text by Brooke Murdock
Illustrations by Amy Bunnell Jones

All right reserved.
For permission requests, email the author at:
bmurdock@dsdmail.net

"ON A FOREVER NATURE WALK WITH D"

-MMM-

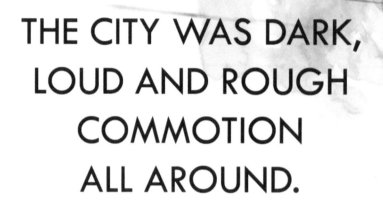

THE CITY WAS DARK,
LOUD AND ROUGH
COMMOTION
ALL AROUND.

WITH INTERNET
STREAMS AND
FLASHING LIGHTS,
CHAOS A
THUNDERING SOUND.

COME MY SON, LETS
SLIP AWAY TO A PLACE
I'LL SHOW TO YOU.

A PLACE WHERE
MEADOW LARKS FLY
FREE, THE SKY A
CRYSTAL BLUE.

NOW TAKE MY HAND
AND WALK WITH ME,
THIS PLACE YOU'LL
COME TO KNOW.

A PLACE MADE BY THE
HAND OF GOD
WHERE PEACEFUL
RIVERS FLOW.

LISTEN, CAN YOU
HEAR IT, THE QUIET
GENTLE BREEZE?

CAN YOU SMELL THE
FRESH COOL AIR
BLOWING SOFTLY
THROUGH THE TREES?

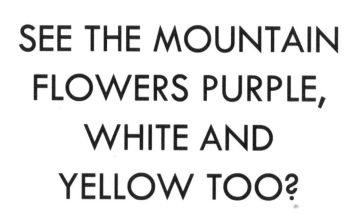

SEE THE MOUNTAIN
FLOWERS PURPLE,
WHITE AND
YELLOW TOO?

THE MIGHTY CLIFFS,
THE ROLLING HILLS,
GOD MADE THEM
ALL FOR YOU.

THE BEAR, THE DEER,
THE CHIPMUNK SMALL,
THE MOOSE SO
LARGE SO GRAND.

A MASTERPIECE
CREATED BY
GOD'S GENTLE
LOVING HAND.

THE MOUNTAINS ARE
SO VAST, SO STILL,
SO WILD, AND FREE.

THEY GIVE US PLACE
TO REST OUR MINDS
MORE BONDED
WE CAN BE.

RETURN TO THESE
MOUNTAINS OFTEN,
LAY DOWN YOUR
SORROWS AND
YOUR CARES.

REMEMBER PEACE
COMES OFTEN TO
THE ONE WHO
TRAVELS THERE.

CPSIA information can be obtained
at www.ICGtesting.com
Printed in the USA
BVHW021208301020
592211BV00003B/5